LAUNDRY

Hints & Tips

LAUNDRY

Hints & Tips

Cindy Harris

RYLAND
PETERS
& SMALL

LONDON NEW YORK

Designer Saskia Janssen
Editor Sharon Cochrane
Picture Researcher Emily Westlake
Production Controller Sheila Smith
Art Director Gabriella Le Grazie
Publishing Director Alison Starling

First published in the
United States in 2005
by Ryland Peters & Small, Inc.
519 Broadway, 5th Floor
New York, NY 10012
www.rylandpeters.com
10 9 8 7 6 5 4 3 2 1

Text © copyright Cindy Harris 2005
Design and photographs ©
copyright Ryland Peters & Small 2005

The text in this book has previously
been published by Ryland Peters &
Small, Inc. in *Keeping House* by
Cindy Harris.

Library of Congress Cataloging-in-
Publication Data

Harris, Cindy, 1947-
  Laundry hints & tips / Cindy Harris.
       p. cm.
  Includes index.
  ISBN 1-84172-847-0
  1. Laundry. I. Title.
TT985H37 2005
648'.1--dc22

                          2004015541

Printed in China

CONTENTS

INTRODUCTION

How inviting it is to climb into a freshly laundered bed or to wrap yourself up in a clean, fluffy towel after luxuriating in the bath. Isn't it far more appealing to have a freshly pressed pile of clothes to choose from in the morning instead of pulling a crumpled shirt off the floor as you rush out the door? These are the easy-to-achieve results that should help transform your laundry routine from a chore into a pleasure.

With little effort you can turn your home into a tactile heaven— sweet-smelling clothes and linens, piles of folded fluffy towels, and crisply pressed shirts—giving results that will make you both proud and satisfied. From washing and drying to ironing and folding, Laundry will help you rediscover these simple pleasures in life.

GETTING STARTED

Bed linen, table linen, towels, and clothes: the laundry can seem a neverending chore. However, if you approach it in a methodical way and have some good accessories to help you, you will start off on the right foot and make the task simple and easier to deal with.

COMING TO GRIPS WITH YOUR LAUNDRY

The best way to deal with your household's laundry, and to maintain your sanity in the process, is to do the majority of the washing on a designated day. That way you won't be burdened with wet shirts, towels, or sheets every single day of the week, and you can tackle the ironing when you have a free half hour.

The Basics

• Schedule a major laundry one day a week. If you have a busy work schedule and you want to keep your weekends free for more pleasurable activities, you may need to do a few loads on some evenings during the week.

• Put a laundry hamper in each bedroom or bathroom.

• Have each member of the household bring his or her washing to a central three-way sorter that separates laundry into lights, darks, and hand-washables. If you have one large hamper for your household's laundry, you will have to sort it before you wash it.

• Separate dry cleaning and put in a closet bag.

• It's always best to treat a stain as soon as possible (see page 32). However, if you are unable to get to the stain immediately, indicate the location of the stain with a safety pin before putting the item in the laundry hamper, so you can find it again easily when you come to treat it.

- If your clothes need hemming, darning, or repairing, do so before washing, because the laundering process may enlarge the tears.
- Do a full load of towels only. This will use less water, less energy, and restrict lint.
- Dry loads one after the other in an automatic dryer to utilize the remaining heat from the previous load.
- Leave lone socks in a collection bag in the laundry room to match with the mate when it eventually turns up.
- Fold clothes before transporting them.
- Keep a few wooden hangers, padded hangers, and rubber-clip hangers handy in the laundry room, so you can hang easily wrinkled items immediately after drying. This will prevent too many wrinkles from forming.
- Return wire hangers to the drycleaner, or throw them out. Don't use them to hang up your clothes because they can ruin the shape of garments.

HOW OFTEN SHOULD YOU LAUNDER?

Try to do a little bit of laundry—whether it's washing, drying, or ironing—twice a week, before it becomes an overwhelming chore. A brimming ironing or laundry hamper is easier to ignore rather than deal with. However, to save fuel and water, wait until you have a full load before firing the washing machine into action.

Daily

• Socks and underwear should be put in the laundry after each use.

• Most other items of clothing can be worn at least twice, as long as there are no stains or odors.

• Dishtowels may need to be changed on a daily basis if you cook frequently for a large family. Otherwise, change them a couple of times a week.

Twice a Week

• Change bath towels.

Once a Week

• Change bed linen once a week, unless the person is ill, in which case you should change it more frequently.

• Toss pillows into a hot tumble dryer for about 15 minutes to freshen them and to eliminate dust mites.

A Few Times a Year

• Launder all bed linens including mattress covers, blankets, pillow covers, quilts, and duvets at least once every three months.

• Turn most frequently used mattresses every four to six months—flip from bottom to top as well as from side to side (you will need help with this). Vacuum the mattresses when you flip them.

• Launder pillows according to the instructions on the labels.

LAUNDRY ACCESSORIES

* Folding *drying rack* or collapsible drying mesh to dry clothes that can't be tumble-dried.

* Rolling *caddy* for product organization.

* *Pant stretchers* to dry pants and make creases.

* *Iron* and *ironing board.*

* *Laundry sorter* and folding table.

* Canvas-covered *collapsible hamper* or laundry organizer.

* *Water alarm*, which will warn you of a possible water leak.

* *Multi-tidy baskets* for sewing kit, shoe polish, spot removers, rags, paper towels, household hint books, and so on.

* *Container* to empty pocket contents into before washing.

* *Bulletin board* for care labels, buttons, stain charts, and product samples.

* *Trash can* for lint.

WASHING

Most of your laundry will be washed in a washing machine, but there will be items in your closet and around your home that need to be washed by hand or professionally drycleaned. Always check the wash care label if you are unsure how an item should be washed.

WASHING MACHINES

There are two types of washing machine: front-loading and top-loading. Front-loading machines consume less energy and less water than their top-loading counterparts. To get the most from your machine, be sure to read the manufacturer's instructions so that you know which settings you have and how they can be used. To get the best results from your machine and the best results for your laundry, follow the simple instructions below.

The Basics

• Select the appropriate program on your machine to correspond with the type of fabric you are washing. Make sure you have selected the right program, temperature, and spin speed, if the controls are separate. Don't forget to check the options available, such as extra rinse, delicate, or rapid wash.

• Load the drum (take care not to over-fill, as performance will be impeded). Turn on the washing machine and let the water in. Add the cleansing products (detergent, bleach, fabric softener, etc.), let them dissolve, then add the laundry.

• Don't machine-wash items that should be hand-washed or drycleaned. Always check the wash care labels on the garments.

• Never overload your machine. An average wash weighs between 5 lb. and 7 lb. for front-loading and top-loading machines respectively.

• Use the proper setting for the size of your load. This is usually indicated on your machine as "small," "medium," or "large" loads.

• For heavy or oily stains, use a liquid prewash treatment first.

• Use a hot water cycle to remove heavy stains (but don't exceed the maximum temperature for the individual items of laundry).

• Use a cool water cycle to reduce shrinking and fading, and to presoak hard-to-remove stains, such as blood and food.

• If you live in a hard-water area, add a water softener to your wash.

• Detergent boosters enhance the performance of the wash in cold water, hard water, or with extra-dirty laundry.

• Use bleach to whiten, brighten, sanitize, and clean your laundry. Chlorine bleach also sanitizes and deodorizes. Always check the wash care label before using.

• Bluing can help remove yellowing on whites.

• Use liquid fabric softener in the final rinse, or a dryer sheet in your automatic dryer to minimize static cling and add softness to the laundry.

• If added crispness is needed, add liquid starch to the final rinse.

• Clean the machine every few months to get clothes cleaner. To do this, fill the machine with hot water, add one cup white vinegar, and let it run through the cycle.

• Check hoses once a year for cracks and bubbles. Replace as needed.

• Clean washer filters periodically and dryer filters after each load.

GUIDE TO WASH CARE SYMBOLS CHART

			Normal wash	Permanent press	Delicate/ gentle	Hand wash	Do not wash
WASHTUB	Washing	MACHINE WASH CYCLES					

			Use any bleach		Use only non-chlorine bleach		Do not bleach
TRIANGLE	Bleaching						

		Hot iron Maximum 390°F	Warm iron Maximum 300°F	Cool iron Maximum 230°
IRON	Ironing			

		Use any solvent	Use any solvent except trichloroethylene	Use petroleum solvent only
CIRCLE	Drycleaning			

			Normal	Permanent press	Delicate/ gentle	Do not tumble dry
SQUARE	Drying	TUMBLE DRYING CYCLE				
		HEAT SETTING	High	Medium	Low	No heat

	MAXIMUM WATER TEMP.					
	200°F	160°F	140°F	120°F	105°F	65°F–85°F
SYMBOL	95°C ⠿	70°C •••	60°C ••	50°C •••	40°C ••	30°C •

Do not iron

Do not steam iron

Do not dryclean

OTHER

Line Dry

Drip Dry

Dry Flat

Do Not Wring

WASHING MACHINE CYCLES

Washing machines are becoming ever-more sophisticated with a huge range of programs and washing options to choose from. However, the following three programs are the most common ones.

Regular Fast agitation, fast spin. This program is suitable for sturdy cotton and linen, and heavily soiled items. It uses hot water for more thorough cleaning. Use strong, all-purpose detergent in this cycle. For extra cleaning of super-soiled clothes, use the presoak option. The double wash option gives the laundry two washes: the first wash skips the middle rinse and removes most of the soil, the second wash goes through the whole cycle. When using this option, it is best to rinse the load again to make sure all the detergent has been removed. Hot water is effective at removing stains most thoroughly, but it can shrink and fade your laundry. Select this program with caution.

Permanent press/wrinkle-free Fast agitation, slow spin, cool-down rinse. This program has less movement than the regular cycle in order to reduce wear on the laundry. It is best used for synthetics, wrinkle-free treated cottons, and blends. It has a cooling-down rinse and cold final rinse for fibers that react to heat. Use more water in this program to reduce friction on fibers: set on "large load" for a medium load, for example. Use a long presoak; there is less agitation on this cycle, so the cleaning is achieved by means of the soaking process. The presoak will loosen dirt and stains for more effective cleansing during the cycle. Be careful with fabric softeners in this cycle—synthetics tend not to absorb them well. It's best to use them in the rinse cycle or dryer.

Delicate or gentle Slow agitation, slow spin, cool water. Unless the care label on your laundry clearly states "dryclean only," this cycle can be used for the following fabrics: silk, wool, viscose, rayon, acrylic, modacrylic, acetate, lace, tulle, and anything sheer, woven, or knitted. Use lingerie detergent in this cycle (available from the lingerie department of a department store). Slow, short movement (6–8 minutes) and spin on the delicate cycle to protect your finest materials from friction and snags.

HAND WASHING

The most delicate fabrics need to be washed by hand rather than in a washing machine (always read the wash care label to check how an item should be washed). It is best to use a specialized detergent for hand washing, which is generally safer for delicate fabrics than most standard detergents. Many department store lingerie sections sell their own brands.

How to Wash by Hand

• Put some cool-to-tepid water in a shallow tub and add some special hand-washing detergent (see the packaging for the recommended amount to use). Immerse the item to be washed in the water and leave to soak for several minutes.

• Gently move the item back and forth through the water.

• Do not squeeze or rub the item.

• Rinse thoroughly in cool clear water.

• Do not wring. Instead, squeeze the excess water out gently by patting the item between two clean, colorfast towels.

• Dry the item flat on a clean towel with no nap or on a hanging rack. If the hanging rack has clips, be sure not to clip the delicate parts of the item or you might stretch or damage it. Instead, just loop the item around the clips.

NON-STANDARD WASHABLES

* Follow the wash care labels to determine whether you *wash by hand*, in a *machine*, or *dryclean*. Always test for colorfastness (see page 32).

* Scrub *plastic shower curtains* with a sponge soaked in a solution made from detergent and hot water. To remove mildew, add a little bleach to the water or use an antimildew spray cleaner. Rinse thoroughly.

* Do not wash *suede* or lined *leather gloves*. Clean the outside with a soft, wet cloth, then clean with a colorless all-purpose conditioner from a shoe or leather goods store.

* *Wool gloves* can be machine washed on a wool cycle or hand washed.

* To hand-wash *lingerie, undergarments,* or *foundations,* see page 25. If these garments can be machine washed, first put delicate items in a mesh lingerie bag and fasten bras to prevent snagging. Wash for five minutes in cold water on a gentle cycle and use lingerie detergent. Select a cool rinse and avoid using chlorine bleach. Dry flat or on a hanging rack.

DETERGENTS, SOAPS, AND OTHER ADDITIVES

Always read the instructions on the detergent and use the cap or measure provided or recommended. When using additives on a garment for the first time, test the fabric for colorfastness (see page 30). The word "free" on a detergent means that nothing has been added to it—no dyes, scents, and so on. "Heavy-duty" and "all-purpose" products can be used on all clothes and linens, except delicates. "Ultra" indicates that the product is concentrated, so only use half the volume of normal detergents.

Mild detergents With a neutral or near-neutral pH, they work less well on stains and heavy dirt than stronger detergents, but they are best for use on delicate fabrics and baby clothes.

Enzyme-based laundry and presoak products These are excellent for getting rid of protein-based spots, such as bodily excretions, dairy products, grass stains, and chocolate. Let the garment soak in the solution for at least one hour before washing as normal.

Fabric softeners These will fluff up the material, remove wrinkles, and reduce static cling. However, with prolonged use, softeners tend to build up in the fibers and eventually become less effective. So use them in limited quantities, and not in every wash. Check the label on the package to see when to add the softener—

some go in a special dispenser, others are added in the final rinse. Don't use fabric softeners on flame-retardant garments, because they reduce the effectiveness of the special treatment.

Optical brighteners These are found in nearly all detergents and all-fabric or oxygen bleaches. After using this product, white or colored material will look crisper and brighter in daylight.

Whiteners/brighteners These are colorless dyes that enhance the appearance of clothes, which can fade or alter color after continued washings. These products can block out the sun, restore color, and whiten whites. They are available separately or as additives to laundry detergents.

Bleach Bleaching is a process by which dark or colored pigments are made to dissolve in the wash. Chlorine bleaches whiten and disinfect material, but can strip fibers and discolor hues. They will damage silk, wool, leather, mohair, nylon, spandex, resin-treated and flame-retardant material. Hydrogen peroxide, in diluted form, is an "oxygen bleach," which is good for fine material, including washable white wool and silk. Oxygen bleach pretreatment sticks are excellent and can be used up to one week before the item is washed. Work the stick into the newly soiled area, then put the item in the hamper until laundry day.

TESTING FOR COLORFASTNESS

When you are washing a garment for the first time, especially a delicate item, always test for colorfastness before washing.

Whites

• Always wash whites separately from colored items to prevent the colors from "bleeding" onto the whites.

• Do not bleach delicate items that specifically state "no bleach."

• Chlorine bleach can bring out crisp whiteness and remove stubborn spots on white clothes.

• If your white clothes have a colored trim, test the trim for color change before using bleach (see opposite).

Colors

• To avoid coloring lighter fabrics, always separate dark colors from light ones before washing.

• Test for possible "bleeding." Materials to test are denim, tie-dyed clothes, hand-painted items, and sari gauzes.

• Fabrics that can continue to bleed are denim, madras, and natural vegetable dyes.

• Always use a detergent recommended for colored fabrics.

Detergent

To check whether a fabric is colorfast with your detergent, do the following test:

1. Add one teaspoon detergent to one cup warm or hot water.

2. Immerse a corner of the garment in the solution.

3. Press onto a clean white cloth, strong paper towel, or tissues.

4. If nothing bleeds, then rinse, let dry, and test again. If the fabric bleeds, or the rag is stained, dryclean the garment.

Chlorine Bleach (Sodium Hypochloride)

To test whether a garment is colorfast with chlorine bleach, carry out this test:

1. Add one tablespoon bleach to one cup water, then apply to a hidden underseam.

2. Wait at least one minute.

3. Dab with a clean white rag.

4. Check for yellowing.

5. After rinsing, dry, then check again.

Other Wash Additives

To test any other washing products, make a slightly stronger solution than normal by mixing it with just a small amount of water. Test as for detergent (see above).

STAIN REMOVAL

Stains are the bane of any laundry washer's life. They can ruin clothes and household linens, but a stain doesn't have to signal the end of a garment's life. There are hundreds of stain-removing products available; it's just a matter of finding the right one.

The Basics

• First check the item to see if it is hand-wash or dryclean only.

• Read and follow package directions on all cleaning products.

• Treat stains as soon as possible, as it is easier to remove new stains that haven't had time to set into the fabric. If the item is dryclean only, take it to be professionally cleaned as soon as you can. Point out the stain to the drycleaner— mark it with a safety pin so you don't forget where on the garment it is.

• Test the stain remover on an unseen area of the item to check for colorfastness exactly as you would a detergent (see page 31). Rinse.

• When using bleach, bleach the entire item to prevent uneven color.

• Place stained material face down on a clean rag or absorbent paper towels when working to remove the stain.

• Put stain remover on the reverse side of the smudge.

• Drycleaning solvents should never go into your washing machine because they are flammable. So, always rinse garments after applying such solvents, and let them air dry before putting them into the washing machine.

• Use stain removers cautiously and separately.

• If there is any bleach in the stain remover, be cautious and check the care label of the material you are treating to see if it is safe to use. If not, try all-purpose or oxygen bleach instead.

• Always wash clothes after you have treated them with stain removers.

COMMON STAINS

The "oops" of eating, the stains from everyday use, the little accidents that happen when we work and play, and the stains that result can ruin our clothes. However, the information given below should give you a fighting chance. If the directions call for bleach, but your fabric is colored, be sure to use a color-safe bleach, which can be found added to many detergents on the market.

Cosmetics

Deodorants, antiperspirants Treat with a liquid detergent; then wash as normal. If more treatment is needed, use a prewash stain remover, then wash with all-fabric bleach.

Foundation Soak the garment using a prewash detergent, then machine wash at as high a temperature as the fabric will allow. For stubborn marks, treat with a stain stick, stain remover, or liquid detergent. Work into the dampened stain until the outline of the stain is gone, then rinse well and wash.

Lipstick Place the garment, stain side down, on paper towels. Sponge dry with cleaning solvent or prewash stain remover. Rub liquid detergent into the stain until its outline fades completely. Launder garment as normal.

Nail polish This is very difficult to remove; try nail-polish remover, but never on synthetics. Place smudged garment, stain side down, on paper towels and soak with nail-polish remover. Replace paper towels frequently as the stain will run into them. Repeat until the stain is gone; rinse, then wash as normal.

Environmental Stains

Grass   Rub with a stain stick or wet with an enzyme product. If this doesn't work, tamp stain down with diluted alcohol. If stain still persists, wash the item in the hottest water allowable for the fabric.

Mud   Let dry, then remove as much of the caked mud as you can. Wash at the hottest temperature allowed for the fabric, and wash with an all-fabric bleach. Repeat the process if necessary.

Pollen   Rub with a damp cloth, then soak in drycleaning solution. Rinse, then let air dry. Gently rub in liquid detergent, then wash with all-fabric bleach.

Everyday Stains

Collar and cuff soils   Apply a stain stick and leave on for one hour, then wash.

Dye transfer (white material that has picked up dye from another garment)
Take out spots with a commercial color-run remover. Wash. If the stain persists, wash again with bleach. For colored fabrics and delicate whites that cannot be bleached, soak in oxygen bleach or an enzyme presoak product, then wash. Note: To minimize dye transfer, remove items from the washing machine as soon as the wash is finished. Wet clothes clumped together can bleed.

Mildew Wash stained items, using bleach. If some soil persists, apply hydrogen peroxide. Rinse and wash again. Let air dry in direct sunlight.

Perspiration Apply a stain remover. Wash in the hottest water allowed for the fabric. Stubborn stains should be pretreated with an enzyme product, then washed with all-fabric bleach.

Yellowing of white cottons or linens Fill your washer with hot water and add a double dose of detergent. Place the item in the washer and spin for four minutes on a regular cycle. Stop the washer and let the garment sit for 15 minutes. Restart the washer and spin for 15 minutes. Complete the wash cycle. Repeat, if necessary.

Yellowing of white nylon Soak the garment overnight in an enzyme presoak product or oxygen bleach. Wash in hot water (check the wash care symbol for the hottest water temperature recommended for the fabric) and add a double dose of bleach.

Foods

Baby formula Soak the stain in an enzyme product for a few hours, then machine wash as normal.

Beverages (sodas, white wine, alcoholic drinks) Soak the stain in tepid water. Rub stain remover or liquid laundry detergent into the spot, then wash with an all-fabric bleach.

Chocolate Treat the stain with an enzyme product. If the stain persists, wash with all-fabric bleach.

Coffee and tea (black or with sugar/sweetener) Run the stain under cool water immediately, if possible; then treat the stain with detergent and wash with all-fabric bleach.

Coffee and tea (with milk or cream only—no sugar) Rub the stain with drycleaning solution. Let air dry. Apply liquid detergent, then wash in the hottest water allowed for that fabric with all-fabric bleach.

Dairy-based products Apply a stain stick to the spot or soak it in an enzyme presoak product for one hour if the stain is recent, or for several hours for older stains. Wash as normal.

Egg Apply an enzyme product to the stain and leave for one hour for a recent stain, or several hours for older stains. Wash as normal.

Fruit juices Soak the item in cool water for 30 minutes. Wash as normal with all-fabric bleach.

Tomato ketchup/sauce Rinse the garment in cold water, then soak in tepid water with ½ cup detergent per gallon of water for about 30 minutes. Spray with stain remover; then wash with all-purpose bleach.

Mustard Apply a prewash stain remover. Wash using chlorine or all-fabric bleach.

Red wine Act immediately. Never cover with salt, which will set the stain. An old wives' antidote is white wine. Soak a clean white rag with white wine and douse the stain liberally with it. Then, with a clean, dry section of the rag, blot dry. You may also try using club soda.

Gum, Paint, and Other Difficult Substances

Chewing gum, adhesive tape First, treat with ice to harden for easy removal; then rub off with the edge of a spatula. Saturate with stain remover. Rinse, then machine wash as normal.

Grease (cooking oil and fats, motor oil) Light soil can be pretreated with a spray stain remover or liquid laundry detergent. Wash in the hottest water allowed for the fabric. Put ingrained spots face down on clean paper towels. Apply cleaning fluid to the back of the stain and change the towels frequently. Let dry; rinse. Wash the garment in the hottest water allowed for the fabric.

Paint Water-based paint, such as latex or acrylic, should be soaked in warm water before the stain sets; then wash. This stain most often can't be treated when dry. For oil-based paints, including varnish, use the solvent listed on the label as thinner. If there is no label information, use turpentine. Rinse. Be sure to use a stain remover, or detergent. Rinse and wash. This is very unlikely to be removed.

Rust Use a commercial rust remover, or a commercial color remover. Treat immediately, because it can spread to other garments.

Shoe polish To remove liquid shoe polish stains, apply a paste of powdered detergent and water, then wash. Use the edge of a spatula to remove any remaining paste and shoe polish from the material. Pretreat with a stain remover; then rinse. Work in detergent to moisten the spot, then wash in chlorine bleach or all-fabric bleach.

Tobacco Wet the spot and work in bar soap; then rinse. Use a stain stick or soak the garment in an enzyme solution; then wash. If the spot persists, wash again using chlorine bleach, if the fabric allows it.

Human Excretions

Blood Let recently stained garments soak in cold water for one hour. Work detergent into the stain. Rinse, then wash. Treat dried spots in lukewarm water with an enzyme product; wash as normal. If stain persists, rewash with bleach.

Urine, vomit, mucus, or feces Treat with an enzyme product. Wash in chlorine bleach or all-fabric bleach. If odor persists, use a fabric deodorizer.

Ink

Ballpoint ink Put the spot face down on a paper towel to absorb most of the stain, then rinse the item and wash as normal. Flush with enough cold water to remove the pigments. Rub liquid detergent into the stain with your fingers, then rinse. Repeat the process, if necessary. Liquid detergents sometimes work. If not, soak in warm water and add one to four tablespoons ammonia per one quart water. Rinse well. Wash in the hottest water allowed for that fabric and use all-fabric bleach.

Felt-tip or India ink Usually indelible, and drawing ink usually cannot be washed out.

Ink Put a drop of water or drycleaning solution on the spot. See which works better.

DRYING

Once you've washed your laundry, spin dry to remove as much water as possible. Line drying will give you the freshest-smelling results, but an automatic tumble dryer is the most convenient method.

AUTOMATIC DRYING

Clean, fresh laundry fluttering in a summer breeze is a romantic sight. But when the weather is wet, the best option for getting your clothes dry is an automatic dryer.

The Basics

• It is best to underdry rather than overdry. Dryers have moisture-sensing strips or "electronic drying" to avoid overdrying and fraying by automatically turning off the machine when the required level of dryness is reached.

• Be sure to place enough clothes in the dryer to provide proper tumbling, but never overfill (only one-third of a full wet load should go into the dryer). You want proper ventilation to provide even drying throughout, without wrinkling.

• Clothes that require specific washing temperatures usually require similar drying temperatures.

• Use regular temperature setting (a hotter setting) for sturdy cottons and preshrunk material.

• Use a medium temperature setting for permanent press and wrinkleproof items.

• Use a low or delicate temperature setting for synthetics, gauzy material, fine knits, anything that will snag, fine lingerie, sheer fabrics, most cotton knits.

• Dryers can wear off elastics and rubber on items such as toilet-seat covers and fitted sheets.

• After every load, check the lint filter and empty it, if necessary. This is really important because too much lint in your dryer can cause a fire. Empty the dryer hose once a year. To do this, remove the hose from the machine and run an old towel through it.

• Remove items from the dryer as soon as the cycle has finished. The items should still have a trace of dampness.

• Hang or fold items as soon as you take them out of the dryer to prevent wrinkles from forming. Have on hand a couple of plastic hangers with molded shoulders, and a place to fold the clothes.

• To condition flat-dried clothes: "air-fluff" them in an automatic dryer on a cool temperature setting. This will prevent them from becoming stiff.

• If clean clothes are wrinkled, put them in the dryer with a moistened, lint-free towel on a low temperature setting for five to ten minutes.

• Tumble dry thick cotton materials to render them fleecy.

DRYING FLAT

* Many knits and woolens have labels indicating that you need to *"lay flat to dry."* If this is the case, make sure you do so; otherwise, you risk *stretching* or *misshaping* the fabric.

* Find a flat area *away from sunlight,* and lay the item flat on a clean, well-pressed white sheet. Make sure the area is *well-ventilated* and *away from pets* and *children*.

* Items dried flat often need to be *"air-dried" for five minutes* in the *automatic dryer* to prevent stiffness. Check the wash care symbol on the garment before putting it in the tumble dryer.

DRIP-DRYING

* *Light cottons, polyesters, silk,* and *items that do not stretch* can be hung to dry. Otherwise, dry flat.

* Hang *jackets, blouses, sweaters* (unless marked "lay flat to dry"), and *dresses* on hangers that fit their shape (not the wire ones from the dry-cleaner), and allow them to drape properly. Make sure the shoulders of the hangers are nicely rounded.

* Be sure to close *buttons* or *snaps* correctly. Smooth *collars, facings, seams, trim,* and *pockets.*

* Use collapsible racks or a hanging rack for *lingerie, hosiery,* and other items that do not need hangers.

LINE DRYING

* Pin *bras* by the hooked end.

* Pin *dresses* by the shoulder.

* Pin *full skirts* by the hem.

* Pin *pillowcases* one side only, leaving the other side to hang open.

* Fold *sheets* hem to hem over the line and pin by the corners.

* Hang *shirts* by the tail, and always unbuttoned.

* Pin *socks* by the toe.

* Pin *straight skirts* and *pants* by the waistband.

* Pin *towels* at the corners, after shaking.

* Pin *t-shirts* by the hem.

* Fold *underwear* over the line and pin.

IRONING & PRESSING

What more pleasing sight is there than a neatly folded pile of freshly ironed clothes and linens? With pristine outfits in your closet, new sheets on the bed, and fresh bathroom and kitchen linens, you will feel revived, and your home will look luxurious once again.

IRONING

There are certain items of clothing and household linen that need to be ironed, while others do not: You can't wear a shirt or finely embroidered blouse that is not ironed, but you can live without linens or sheets being ironed—although this can be one of life's little luxuries!

The Basics

• Make sure your ironing board is well padded.

• Your iron should be rust-free and have a clean tank with no mineral deposits (see page 57).

• Wait until the iron is hot enough to steam the water before starting to iron.

• Always use the correct temperature setting for the particular item (check the wash care label).

• Test the heat on a hidden area of material, such as the underside of a hem, to avoid scorching your garments.

• Put the item on the ironing board and flatten it out.

• Use one hand to keep the garment in a fixed position while the other hand moves the iron.

• Move the iron deliberately in a sliding motion over the fabric, applying only light pressure to it.

• Never leave the hot plate of the iron facing downward. Always set the iron on its stand when you let it rest.

• Iron garments needing the lowest setting first, and progress to those needing the highest. Use the one-dot setting for nylon, acetate, silk, rayon, acrylic, and polyester; the two-dot setting for permanent press, polyester/cotton blends, and wool; the three-dot setting for cotton, linen, and denim.

• Iron thicker areas of the garment first to avoid rewrinkling the thinner, more delicate parts as you continue to iron the rest of the garment.

• Have on hand a sprinkler or spray bottle or a sponge for sprinkling water, and spray starches and/or spray sizing. Keep these in a handy caddy.

• Cottons and linens should be sprinkled with water one hour before ironing. Press while still damp, using a hot steam iron setting. Flatwork should be sprinkled on one side only. Two-sided items, such as clothing and pillowcases, should be sprinkled on both sides.

• Use a steam-iron setting on untreated cottons, rayons, and silks.

• Use a dry iron on permanent press and synthetic fabrics.

• For minimum ironing, use permapress clothes and blended fabrics. Remove from the dryer as soon as the cycle has finished, fluff out, and fold or hang neatly.

• Always hang or fold laundry as soon as it is dry to minimize the creases and therefore reduce your ironing load.

PRESSING

Delicate fabrics should be pressed rather than ironed to prevent them from getting crushed, stretched, or damaged, or becoming shiny. Tailored suits as well as garments made from wool, silk, rayon, net, and pile fabrics should all be pressed.

The Basics

• Whereas ironing involves "sliding" the iron across the fabric, pressing comprises a press-and-lift technique. Press the iron onto the fabric, then lift it off quickly; avoid "sliding" the iron as much as possible.

• A pressing cloth should be used to act as a heat buffer between the iron and the fabric. This can be made from unbleached muslin or cheesecloth, or you can use a clean white towel.

• When pressing delicate fabrics, put a heavy towel (without a nap) under the item. Press on the wrong side of the fabric, using a steam iron setting or a damp pressing cloth, and your iron set at medium heat.

• Wrinkles should be steamed out.

IRONING TIPS

Here are some helpful hints to consider when ironing a variety of fabrics or garments with decorative features.

Creases Iron on the wrong side first, using small strokes on collars, hems, and cuffs, while pressing out smoothly with the palm of your hand.

Damasks Iron both sides to produce a sheen on the top side.

Delicate fabrics To avoid creating a sheen on delicate fabrics, iron on the wrong side or use a clean towel as a pressing cloth. This applies to fabrics such as wool gabardine, polyester, linen, and all silks.

Embroidered or sequined fabrics Lay the item face down on a cotton dishtowel; then iron on the wrong side with a pressing cloth over the top of the fabric to protect patterns and delicacies.

Fringes Untangle while wet.

Gathers Iron from the outside into the gathered edge.

Lace and cutwork Use a pressing cloth or dishtowel; don't put the iron directly on the lace.

Linen Sprinkle linen items with water, then stretch the damp linen into shape. Use a hot iron, but take care because linen can scorch quite easily. Iron the garment on the wrong side to press it into shape, but not to dry it. Stop ironing while there is still a suggestion of dampness in the fabric. Overdrying will increase the chance of scorching. Never iron on the right side. Hang immediately to finish drying naturally.

Napkins Iron flat. Do not iron creases, these should be pressed instead.

Pile fabrics These fabrics should not be ironed.

Plackets Close zippers, snaps, and hooks, but not buttons, before ironing plackets. Work the iron carefully around any buttons, hooks, snaps, or zippers.

Pleats Lay or pin the pleats in place before ironing. Hold the material taut against the pressure of the iron. Iron in long strokes starting at the waist and working down to the hem.

Puffed sleeves Stuff puffed sleeves or pockets with tissue paper or a small towel before ironing.

Sheets Fold flat sheets in half; iron, then fold completely. There is no need to iron fitted sheets because they are pulled tightly over the corners of the mattress and any creases will disappear.

Stretchy fabrics Put a pressing cloth on top of the fabric and iron in the direction of the weave.

Tablecloths Iron round ones in a circular motion, turning the fabric around as you iron. Fold square or rectangular ones in half, wrong side facing out. Sprinkle with water, then iron until half-dry; refold with right side facing out, then iron on the right side until nearly dry. Press out any creases when both sides are finished.

IRON CARE

* Let your iron *air-dry to cool*. Give it plenty of time to cool and don't be impatient.

* If starch adheres to the soleplate, wait for the iron to cool completely, then apply a mixture of *one part baking soda* to *one part water*. Leave for 15 minutes, then work off with a moist rag. Alternatively, use a commercial soleplate cleaner.

* Mineral deposits develop with time inside the iron's water tank. To remove them, pour some *white vinegar* inside and *allow the iron to steam* for *five minutes*, but check the manufacturer's instructions first. Iron a clean rag to bring out any residues. Let the iron cool, then rinse the tank with cold water.

* Always empty the water out after each use.

* If you use *tap water* in your iron, you will accelerate the buildup of mineral deposits. Prevent this by using only distilled water.

* Clean any *anti-deposit* devices as recommended by the manufacturer.

FOLDING

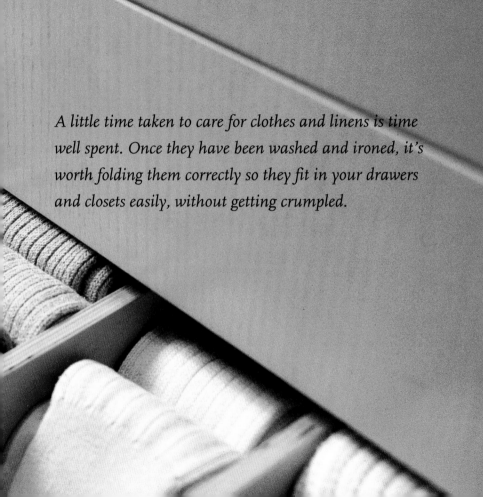

A little time taken to care for clothes and linens is time well spent. Once they have been washed and ironed, it's worth folding them correctly so they fit in your drawers and closets easily, without getting crumpled.

CLOTHING

If you fold your clothes carefully, you will set the creases in the right places and prevent them from getting wrinkled in your drawers or on your shelves. Follow the simple instructions below to achieve the best results for your clothes.

Dresses   It is advisable to hang dresses in a closet. But if you can't, fold them at the waist, then tuck the sleeves in like a shirt (see below). Bring the edges of the skirt together carefully. If the skirt is long, fold it up, but not in the middle.

Handkerchiefs   Fold handkerchiefs in a square after pressing.

Lingerie   Divide into three separate drawers—or into three separate compartments within a large drawer—one for panties, one for brassieres, and one for hosiery. Panties should be separated by color and folded like underpants (see opposite). Brassieres should be stored by color and kept uncrushed, cup-side up. Store previously worn hose according to color and thickness and fold into fourths. Keep scented sachets in your lingerie drawer to keep it sweet-smelling.

Pants and slacks   Use skirt hangers. Hang them carefully by the hems, making sure to align the inseams. If you don't have skirt hangers, use thick, wooden hangers and fold them over the hanger, making sure to align the inseams.

Shirts   Button first, middle, and last buttons or snaps and set the shirt face down. Bring one sleeve across the back of the shirt horizontally, folding the shoulder over, too. Fold the sleeve down vertically at the shoulder area. Repeat with the other sleeve. Fold the lower third up, then fold the next third up. Turn the shirt face up. Put away carefully in a drawer or on a shelf.

Shorts First, carefully flatten any pockets. Align the inseams and try to lay the shorts out evenly in a drawer. If you must fold them, do so carefully in half.

Skirts It is always better to hang a skirt, either in a clip hanger or by its own loops. If you cannot, bring the edges of the skirt together. If the skirt is long, fold it up, but avoid folding it in the middle.

Socks Never roll up into a ball. This stretches one sock, ruining its elastic and takes up too much room in the drawer. Instead, put one sock on top of the other and fold them neatly together in half.

Underpants Lay them out flat. Fold each side toward the middle, then fold them up in half.

HOUSEHOLD LINEN

When folding more sizeable items, such as sheets, blankets, and large tablecloths, the task is made much easier and the result is much neater with two people. If you do have to do it on your own, lay the items on the bed and fold them there.

Blankets Fold in half from bottom to top, then in half from left to right. Flip the blanket over and fold again.

Duvet/comforter To store, put the comforter in washed, unbleached muslin or cotton. Use tissue paper between the folds and store in an acid-free box or on a shelf lined with cotton sheeting. You can buy storage bags for duvets and blankets. Never use plastic bags, because they lock in moisture. To prevent mold and mildew, duvets must not be stored in a humid room, such as the bathroom. Heating units and direct sunlight can ruin your duvet.

Fitted sheets Make sure both top corners of the sheet are puffed out. Fold the sheet in half from bottom to top. Fit the two bottom corners into the two top corners. Make the sides of the sheet perfectly even by laying it flat on the bed and smoothing down. Fold in half again from bottom to top, then from left to right. Lay the sheet neatly on a shelf, tamping down in order to prevent any wrinkles from forming.

Flat sheets Match the bottom edges to the top edges and fold in half, with the right side of the sheet facing out. Fold in half from bottom to top again, then fold from left to right. Larger sheets may need to be folded from bottom to top one more time so that they fit on the shelf. Tamp down. Lay your fitted sheets on top of your flat sheets.

Napkins Like tablecloths, store these in an acid-free container or on shelves papered with cotton sheeting. Never iron creases, or mold may develop. Fold loosely into a square or rectangle, with the monogram or motif (if applicable) on the lower left-hand corner. You may also fold into a triangular shape, with the monogram at the base of the triangle.

Pillowcases Fold in half lengthwise, then in half widthwise.

Tablecloths Store linen tablecloths wrapped in acid-free paper. Keep either in an acid-free container or on shelves papered with cotton sheeting. Be sure to refold frequently to prevent mold and creasing.

Towels Fold in thirds lengthwise, then in half or thirds widthwise.

INDEX

PICTURE CREDITS

ph = photographer

Endpapers ph Jan Baldwin; 1 ph Catherine Gratwicke/designer Caroline Zoob's workroom (+44 (0)1273 479274 for commissions); 2 ph Debi Treloar/Mark and Sally of Baileys Home and Garden's house, Herefordshire (+44 (0)1989 563015, www.baileyshomeandgarden.com); 3 ph Andrew Wood; 4 ph Jan Baldwin/Sophie Eadie's family home, London; 6 & 8–9 ph Debi Treloar/inset the home of Patty Collister, London, owner of An Angel At My Table (+44 (0)20 7424 9777); 10–11 ph Polly Wreford; 12 ph Jan Baldwin; 15 ph Catherine Gratwicke/retro laundry bags from The Laundry (+44 (0)20 7274 3838); 16–17 ph Debi Treloar/Mark and Sally of Baileys Home and Garden's house, Herefordshire(+44 (0)1989 563015, www.baileyshomeandgarden.com); 22–23 ph Tom Leighton; 24 ph Simon Upton/Lena Proudlock's house, Gloucestershire (www.lenaproudlock.com); 27 ph Christopher Drake/designer Barbara Davis' own house, upstate New York (607 264 3673); 28–32 ph Debi Treloar; 39–37 ph Henry Bourne; 38–39 ph Alan Williams; 40–41 ph Christopher Drake/Tita Bay's village house, Ramatuelle (+39 03 52 58 384); 45–49 ph Polly Wreford; 50–51 ph Polly Eltes; 52 ph Andrew Wood; 54–55 ph Sandra Lane; 56 ph Andrew Wood; 58–59 ph Chris Everard/"Manhattan Loft" designed by Bruce Bierman Design, Inc. (212-243-1935 www.biermandesign.com); 60–61 ph Chris Everard; 62–63 ph David Loftus